ON THE ANVIL

ON THE ANVIL

MAX LUCADO

Tyndale House
Publishers, Inc.
Wheaton, Illinois

Library of Congress Catalog Card Number 85-50732
ISBN 0-8423-4738-0
©1985 by Max Lucado
Printed in the United States of America
95 94 93 92 91
18 17 16 15 14 13

To my mother and father,
two people who have the courage
of a giant and the heart of a child

CONTENTS

PART THREE: AN INSTRUMENT
FOR NOBLE PURPOSES

CONCLUSION: EMERGING FROM THE ANVIL

With tenderest appreciation to:

Doug and Carl—for three unforgettable Gold Coast years.

Stanley, Landon, and Lynn—for helping the Word become an action verb.

Steve and Cheryl—for your unquenchable loyalty.

Fern, Sue, and Laurie—for keeping your eyes on my grammar and your fingers on the typewriter.

And, most of all, my lifelong partner Denalyn. If every man had a wife like you, how sweet the world would be!

INTRODUCTION: THE BLACKSMITH'S SHOP

In the shop of a blacksmith, there are three types
of tools. There are tools on the junkpile:
outdated,
broken,
dull,
rusty.
They sit in the cobwebbed corner, useless to their
master, oblivious to their calling.

There are tools on the anvil:
melted down,
molten hot,
moldable,
changeable.
They lie on the anvil, being shaped by their master,
accepting their calling.

There are tools of usefulness:
sharpened,
primed,

defined,
mobile.
They lie ready in the blacksmith's toolchest, available to their master, fulfilling their calling.

Some people lie useless:
lives broken,
talents wasting,
fires quenched,
dreams dashed.
They are tossed in with the scrap iron, in desperate need of repair, with no notion of purpose.

Others lie on the anvil:
hearts open,
hungry to change,
wounds healing,
vision clearing.
They welcome the painful pounding of the blacksmith's hammer, longing to be rebuilt, begging to be called.

Others lie in their Master's hands:
well-tuned,
noncompromising,
polished,
productive.
They respond to their Master's forearm, demanding nothing, surrendering all.

We are all somewhere in the blacksmith's shop. We are either on the scrap pile, on the anvil, in the Master's hands, or in the toolchest. (Some of us have been in all three.)

In this collection of writings we'll take a tour of the "shop." We'll examine all tools and look in all corners. From the shelves to the workbench, from the water to the fire. . . .

And I'm sure that somewhere you'll see yourself. We'll discover what Paul meant when he spoke of becoming "an instrument for noble purposes." And what a "becoming" it is! The rubbish pile of broken tools, the anvil of recasting, the hands of the Master—it's a simultaneously joyful and painful voyage.

And for you who make the journey—who leave the heap and enter the fire, dare to be pounded on God's anvil, and doggedly seek to discover your own purpose—take courage, for you await the privilege of being called "God's chosen instruments."

—*Max Lucado, Rio de Janeiro, Brazil*

PART ONE
THE PILE OF
BROKEN TOOLS

ONE
THE PILE OF
BROKEN TOOLS

"To find me, look in the corner of the shop,
    over here,
        behind the cobwebs,
        beneath the dust,
           in the darkness.
There are scores of us,
    broken handles,
      dulled blades,
        cracked iron.
Some of us were useful once, and then . . .
    many of us never were.
But, listen, don't feel sorry for me.
Life ain't so bad here in the pile . . .
    no work,
      no anvils,
        no pain,
          no sharpening,
and yet, the days are very long."

TWO
I AM VERY WEARY

It will be remembered as one of the most confounding missing-persons cases.

In August of 1930, forty-five-year-old Joseph Crater waved good-bye to friends after an evening meal in a New York restaurant, flagged down a taxi, and rode off. He was never seen or heard from again.

Fifty years of research have offered countless theories but no conclusions. Since Crater was a successful New York Supreme Court judge, many have suspected murder, but a solid lead has never been found. Other options have been presented: kidnapping, Mafia involvement, even suicide.

A search of his apartment revealed one clue. It was a note attached to a check, and both were left for his wife. The check was for a sizable amount and the note simply read, "I am very weary. Love, Joe."

The note could have been nothing more than a thought at the end of a hard day. Or it could have meant a great deal more—the epitaph of a despairing man.

Weariness is tough. I don't mean the physical weariness that comes with mowing the lawn, or the mental weariness that follows a hard day of decisions and thinking. No, the weariness that attacked Judge Crater is much worse. It's the weariness that comes just before you give up. That feeling of honest desperation. It's the dispirited father, the abandoned child, or the retiree with time on his hands. It's that stage in life when motivation disappears; the children grow up, a job is lost, a wife dies. The result is weariness—deep, lonely, frustrated weariness.

Only one man in history has claimed to have an answer for it. He stands before all the Joseph Craters of the world with the same promise: "Come to me, all you who are weary . . . and I will give you rest" (Matt. 11:28).

THREE
NOW, DON'T GET CARRIED AWAY!

"Peter followed at a distance"
(Luke 22:54).

Peter was sharp.
>He kept his distance from Jesus.
>"I'll stay close enough to see him," Peter reasoned.
>"But not too close, or I may get caught."

Good thinking, Peter.
>Don't get too involved—it might hurt.
>Don't be too loyal—you might get branded.
>Don't show too much concern—they'll crucify you, too.

We need more men like you, Peter.
>Men who keep religion in its place.
>Men who don't stir the water.
>Men who reek with mediocrity.

That's the kind of man God needs, yessir.
>One who knows how to keep his distance:
>"Now, I'll pay my dues and I'll come once a week,

but . . . well . . . you can get carried away,
you know."

Yes, you can get carried away . . .
    up a hill
      to a cross
      —and killed.

Peter learned a lesson that day—a hard lesson.
    It is better never to have followed Jesus, than
    to have followed him and denied him.

Mark these words—
    Follow at a distance and you'll deny the Mas-
    ter. Period.
    You won't die for a man you can't touch.
    Period.
    But stay near to him, in his shadow. . . .
    You'll die with him, gladly.

FOUR
NEW WINE IS FOR
FRESH SKINS
Mark 2:22

I'll never forget Steven. I met him in St. Louis. His twenty-three years had been hard on him, his arm scarred from the needle and his wrist scarred from the knife. His pride was his fist and his weakness was his girl.

Steve's initial response to love was beautiful. As we unfolded the story of Jesus before him, his hardened face would soften and his dark eyes would dance.

He wanted to change.

But his girl friend would have none of it. Oh, she would listen politely and would be very sweet, but her heart was gripped by darkness. Any changes Steve made would be quickly muffled as she would craftily maneuver him back into his old habits. She was the last thing between him and the Kingdom. We begged him to leave her. He was trying to put new wine into an old wineskin.

He wrestled for days trying to decide what to do. Finally, he reached a conclusion. He couldn't leave her.

The last time I saw Steve he wept . . . uncontrollably. I held big, tough, macho Steve in my arms. The prophecy of Jesus was true. By putting his new wine into an old skin, it was lost.

Think for a minute. Do you have any wineskins that need to be thrown out? Look closely in your closet. They come in all sizes. Maybe yours is an old indulgence—food, clothes, sex; or an old habit, like gossip or profanity. Or possibly, like Steve, an old relationship. No friendship or romance is worth your soul. Repentance means change. And change means purging your heart of anything that can't coexist with Christ.

You can't put new life into an old life-style. The inevitable tragedy occurs. The new life is lost.

FIVE
SOUR GRAPES

I once knew a man who treated Bible class and the worship service like a harsh movie critic treats a new release.
"Entertain me!"
Arms folded.
Lips tight.
Expectant.
"This had better be good."

With a ruthless eye and a critical ear
he sat
and watched
and listened.

The teacher, the minister, the music director: all were his prey. And woe be unto the teacher who didn't ask his opinion, unto the minister who went a few minutes over, unto the music director who chose songs the critic didn't know.

I once knew a man who came every Sunday to be entertained and not to encourage. He remarked that the Sunday afternoon game was more exciting than the Sunday morning assembly.

I wasn't surprised.

SIX
BILLIE RESIGNS

One evening in 1954 Billie Sicard resigned from life. No official announcement was made and no papers were signed. But still, she resigned. For all practical purposes, Billie decided to live no longer. Her spirit died in 1954; her body died in 1979.

On that evening in 1954, Billie's only reason to live left her. Her twelve-year-old son, George, died of a brain tumor. Little George's death left Billie prisoned inside a vacuum. She had been thirty-four when she had borne him. After her husband left, little George became her life. When he died, his death became hers.

She was well-to-do. Billie had lived on exclusive Sunset Island in Miami since 1937. After her death, the house went at an auctioned price of $226,000. Yet all this was immaterial to Billie. Her life had been her child.

They say that after George died in a New York City hospital, the body was brought to her home for a wake. After displaying the body for a day in the home of Mrs. Sicard, the funeral director came to remove it. She refused to let him. For several days she mourned behind locked doors before she gave the body up.

It had been nothing for Billie to go on a shopping spree and spend $100 on toys for George. In 1979 when her body was found, so were the toys, exactly as her son had left them. Nothing was packed, nothing moved. For twenty-five years Billie had roamed in a house full of toys with a heart full of memories. When the house was sold after her death, little George's Cub Scout uniform was still hanging in the downstairs coat closet. On the wall was a child's sketch of a choo-choo train drawn in red crayon. She had never washed it off. His Mickey Mouse slippers sat in the corner of his bedroom. In the garage sat a 1941 Packard, a gift she had given to little George on his tenth birthday.

When Billie resigned from life, she became a social recluse. Her yard became a jungle. Her home became a source of ghost stories and old wives' tales. She overate. She withdrew. She didn't care.

Billie resigned.

Her life stands as a quiet legacy to us all. Man must have something larger than death . . . or death takes man.

SEVEN
FOR THE LOVE OF
A STRANGER AND
THE LACK OF A
NAME

John's life peaked at age thirteen, when he was homeroom president. So far, that office has been the high point in his life.

John's life is an enigma. Though he was born in a $300,000 home, he is known as a penniless drifter. Though he is the son of a successful oil tycoon, John quits more things than he finishes. Though his parents are gregarious and social, John is introverted, reclusive, almost stoic.

Friends suggest that he became a victim of his own failures. In a family of successes he had made no name for himself. His brother and sister made it, but he didn't. The black sheep. The family failure. He had no name.

"Everything fits perfectly . . . except John," one friend observed about the family.

College only added to the degeneration. He attended on and off for seven years, never graduating. John was a loner at school, a lumpish young man with glassy eyes and a glower. One of the professors recalls, "There were usually empty chairs around him, as if he consciously chose to sit apart."

We don't know what emotions stirred within John. Anger, perhaps, at a society that only reminded him of his inadequacies. Guilt. Painful reminders that "I let everybody down." Nothingness. Barely known by those he touched, his passage was marked only by clutter and grime and confused scribbling.

We don't know the emotions, but we believe we know their result.

John Hinckley, Jr., seemed to have had every intention of killing the President. For the love of a stranger and the lack of a name, he allegedly emptied a revolver into the bodies of four men.

The latest report has John in a federal correctional facility in North Carolina. His room has a sink, toilet, single bed, one bulletproof window, and no TV or radio. He tried to overdose on Tylenol, and failed. John can't kill a president, nor can he kill himself.

Our world has little room for failures. Our success-centered enterprise system is ideal for the successful, but devastating for the loser. In an effort to create winners, we also create misfits.

Jesus had a place for misfits. In his book, the last became first, and even the loser had value. It is our responsibility to be like Christ. It is our responsibility to intercept a life like John Hinckley's and fill it with value.

EIGHT
MERCY, NOT
SACRIFICE
Matthew 9:13

"Lord," I said, "I want to be your man, not my
  own.
So to you I give my money, my car—even my
  home."

Then, smug and content, I relaxed with a smile
And whispered to God, "I bet it's been a while,
Since anyone has given so much—so freely?"
His answer surprised me. He replied, "Not really."

"Not a day has gone by since the beginning of time,
That someone hasn't offered meager nickels and
  dimes,
Golden altars and crosses, contributions and pe-
  nance,
Stone monuments and steeples; but why not repentance?

"The money, the statues, the cathedrals you've
  built,
Do you really think I need your offerings of guilt?

What good is money that's meant only to salve
The hurting conscience that so many of you have?

"Your lips know no prayers. Your eyes, no com-
passion.
But you will go to church (when churchgoing's in
fashion).

"Just give me a tear—a heart ready to mold.
And I'll give you a mission, a message so bold—
That a fire will be stirred where there was only
death,
And your heart will be flamed by my life and my
breath."

I stuck my hands in my pockets and kicked at the
dirt.
It's tough to be corrected (I guess my feelings were
hurt).
But it was worth the struggle to realize the thought.
That the cross isn't for sale and Christ's blood can't
be bought.

NINE
WHO IS
RIGHTEOUS?

Question: Oh, Lord, who shall live in your tent?
Answer: He who does what is right (Ps. 15:1).

Have you ever noticed how many people want to
be right before God?
>   Rich people,
>   Religious people,
>   Nature people,
>   City people.

All kinds of people want to be right.

Some people get educated:
>   they learn all the funny little Greek symbols,
>   they learn all about theology,
>   they learn all about manuscripts, papyri,
>   Dead Sea scrolls,
>   and so on and on. . . .

They are righteous, they say . . . and they huddle
together and sneer at those who are not.

Some people get mission-minded:
    they learn new languages,
    they teach untaught people,
    they take pictures of converts and speak at
    conferences.

They are righteous, they say . . . and they all huddle together and sneer at those who are not.

Some people get vocational:
    they get a job,
    they pay their own way,
    they rub elbows with the "real world,"
    they are drops of leaven in a swelling society.

They are righteous, they say . . . and they all huddle together and sneer at those who are not.

You know, I think that sometimes God looks down
    at this dusty footstool and sees
      the righteous theological huddle,
        the righteous missionary huddle,
        the righteous vocational huddle
        . . . and I think he sighs.

TEN
HOPE FOR LEO?

Let me introduce you to Leo.

I used to eat breakfast at a Cuban restaurant near my house. It was a brief, brisk walk and a good opportunity to think out my plans for the day. My thoughts were interrupted one morning, however, by a spry, unabashed old gent sporting a golf cap and dirty work pants. (He didn't look his sixty-six years.)

"You a student, son?" (I guess he saw my Bible and notebook.) "I've got some college textbooks for sale." I followed him into an empty house cluttered with lamps, books, end tables, all for sale. He was moving, he explained. "I need to get rid of this stuff." One topic led to another. Soon we were sitting and talking, Leo with his questions about the Pope, the Bible, and "souls"; and me with my questions about Leo.

His history was colorful: "a Depression kid"; sold franks at Yankee Stadium and programs at Madison Square Garden; a taxi driver in Miami. Yet although his life was full of experience, his face was void of joy. He spoke of how "you can't trust nobody no more. It's a hard world." When I tried to leave, he insisted that I stay. He was hungry for conversation. His fifth and last child had just left home. He said nothing about his marriage, though family portraits covered the wall. "I want to move . . . somewhere," he mumbled. Leo was in that era of life when all you have to look forward to is death and all you have to look back on is memories. To Leo, life was very real. To Leo, life was very empty.

Maybe it was unfair that I ask such a painful question, but I asked it anyway: "If you could live life all over again, would you?"

He looked at me and then at the floor. "No," he said sadly, "I don't think so."

It's hard to be without light in a dark world.

ELEVEN
JUDAS, THE MAN
WHO NEVER KNEW

I've wondered, at times, what kind of man this Judas was. What he looked like, how he acted, who his friends were.

I guess I've stereotyped him. I've always pictured him as a wiry, beady-eyed, sly, wormy fellow, pointed beard and all. I've pictured him as estranged from the other apostles. Friendless. Distant. Undoubtedly he was a traitor and a quisling. Probably the result of a broken home. A juvenile delinquent in his youth.

Yet I wonder if that is so true. We have no evidence (save Judas's silence) that would suggest that he was isolated. There is little reason to believe that Judas was dishonest. In fact, Judas was in charge of the treasury. One wouldn't hand the money over to a distrustful soul. At the Last Supper, when Jesus said that his betrayer sat at the table, we don't find the apostles immediately turning to Judas as the logical traitor.

No, I think we've got Judas pegged wrong. Perhaps he was just the opposite. Instead of sly and wiry, maybe he was robust and jovial. Rather than quiet and introverted, he could have been outgoing and well-meaning. I don't know.

But for all the things we don't know about Judas, there is one thing we know for sure: he had no relationship with the Master. He had seen Jesus, but he did not know him. He had heard Jesus, but he did not understand him. He had a religion, but no relationship.

As Satan worked his way around the table in the Upper Room, he needed a special kind of man to betray our Lord. He needed a man who had seen Jesus, but who did not know him. He needed a man who knew the actions of Jesus, but had missed out on the mission of Jesus. Judas was this man. He knew the empire but had never known the Man.

We learn this timeless lesson from the betrayer. Satan's best tools of destruction are not from outside the church, they are within the church. A church will never die from the immorality in Hollywood or the corruption in Washington. But it will die from corrosion within—from those who bear the name of Jesus but have never met him, and from those who have religion, but no relationship.

Judas bore the cloak of religion, but he never knew the heart of Christ. Let's make it our goal to know . . . deeply.

TWELVE
THE HOPE THAT
WENT IGNORED

Once upon a time there was a tiny hamlet in the Swiss Alps. This hamlet was in serious trouble. The well that supplied water to the village went dry. The people began to panic. A river was near the community, but it was located at the bottom of a deep, deep gorge; hence, no one could reach the water. And it was the middle of summer, so the snow on the mountain had long since melted.

There was, however, another well flowing with water across the gorge on the adjacent mountainside. An imaginative young thinker came up with a solution. He built a bridge across the gorge.

The villagers were elated.

A bucket brigade was formed immediately and the water supply was replenished. Needless to say, the bridge became very important to this group. It was their source of life.

They honored the bridge. They named the bridge after the builder and painted it a beautiful gold. Tinsel was strung from the bridge. Miniature bridges were built and sold in the streets. People wore them on their necks and hung them in the windows. A committee was formed to pay homage to the bridge. Only certain people were allowed upon it, and then only on certain days, and then only when wearing certain clothes. The bridge keeper became the most respected and revered position on the mountain. No one could see or cross the bridge without his permission.

Unfortunately, there were disputes within the committee. The disagreement centered around whether a canopy should be built over the bridge. So the bridge was closed until a decision could be made.

Many villagers died of thirst while the leaders debated.

In the search for truth, the means often become the end.

THIRTEEN
EYES THAT NEVER
SEE; EARS THAT
NEVER HEAR

He's a deadly snake. Mark my words. Satan's snake. Be on your guard.

He's sly and wily. He lurks in every dark corner and musty hole. He strikes with abandon. The old, the rich, the poor, the young—all are his prey. He worms his way into every life and seldom misses his target.

And what slyness! We never know when he will strike. When he will creep up, we never know. All we see are the results of his deadly bite: blank faces, nonreflective hearts, questionless minds, empty lives. A trail cluttered with broken hearts and tears.

Who is this snake? Greed? Lust? Egotism? No (even though they are just as deadly). No, I'm unmasking the vilest of hell's vipers—complacence.

Complacence. Life with no questions. Blind acceptance. No probing. No searching. No yearning.

We live in a world plagued by complacence.

We are complacent to hope. Many people settle for a stale, vanilla life-style that peaks at age seventeen. Hope? What's to hope for? Life is a paycheck and a weekend. Nothing more. You'd think we all had blinders. It's like one car after another driving off a cliff, no one daring to object. Like watercolor names painted on a sidewalk . . . washing away in an August rain.

We're complacent to death. Masked faces at a funeral endure the procession; weep at the burial. And then, a few hours later, giggle at Johnny Carson. "The only way to handle death is to accept it as inevitable. Don't question it or defy it. You'll walk away depressed. Close your eyes. Put your hands over your ears. There is no explanation." We stand complacent.

Complacent to God. Churchgoers pack the pews and sing to the back of someone's head. Fellowship is lost in formality. One, two, three times a week people pay their dues by walking in the door, enduring a ritual, and walking out. Guilt is appeased. God is insulted. Are we so naive as to think that he needs our attendance? Are we so ignorant that we put God in a box, thinking he can be taken in and out at our convenience?

Complacent to purpose. How in the world can a person be born, be educated, fall in or out of love, have a job, be married, give birth, raise kids, see death, cry, scream, giggle, drink, eat, smoke, climb up or down the ladder, retire, and die without ever, ever asking why? Never asking, "Why am I here?" Or, worse yet, asking why and being content with no answer. History is jam-packed with lives that died with no purpose. Neighborhoods reek with mediocrity. Office complexes are painted gray with boredom. Nine-to-fivers are hypnotized by routine.

But does anyone object? Does anyone defy the machinery? Does anyone ask why?

Sometimes I want to stand at the corner of the street and yell, "Doesn't anyone want to know why? Why lonely evenings? Why broken hearts? Why abandoned marriages? Why fatherless babies?" But I never yell it. I just stick my hands in my pockets and stare . . . and wonder.

The most deadly trick of Satan is not to rob us of answers. It's to steal our questions.

PART TWO
ON THE ANVIL

FOURTEEN
ON THE ANVIL

With a strong forearm, the apron-clad blacksmith puts his tongs into the fire, grasps the heated metal, and places it on his anvil. His keen eye examines the glowing piece. He sees what the tool is now and envisions what he wants it to be—sharper, flatter, wider, longer. With a clear picture in his mind, he begins to pound. His left hand still clutching the hot mass with the tongs, the right hand slams the two-pound sledge upon the moldable metal.

On the solid anvil, the smoldering iron is remolded.

The smith knows the type of instrument he wants. He knows the size. He knows the shape. He knows the strength.

Wang! Wang! The hammer slams. The shop rings with noise, the air fills with smoke and the softened metal responds.

But the response doesn't come easily. It doesn't come without discomfort. To melt down the old and recast it as new is a disrupting process. Yet the metal remains on the anvil, allowing the toolmaker to remove the scars, repair the cracks, refill the voids, and purge the impurities.

And, with time, a change occurs: what was dull becomes sharpened; what was crooked becomes straight; what was weak becomes strong; and what was useless becomes valuable.

Then the blacksmith stops. He ceases his pounding and sets down his hammer. With a strong left arm, he lifts the tongs until the freshly molded metal is at eye level. In the still silence he examines the smoking tool. The incandescent implement is rotated and examined for any mars or cracks.

There are none.

Now the smith enters the final stage of his task. He plunges the smoldering instrument into a nearby bucket of water. With a *hiss* and a rush of smoke, the metal immediately begins to harden. The heat surrenders to the onslaught of cool water and the pliable, soft mineral becomes an unbending, useful tool.

". . . for a little while you may have had to suffer grief in all kinds of trials. These have come so that your faith—of greater worth than gold, which perishes even though refined by fire—may be proved genuine and may result in praise, glory and honor when Jesus Christ is revealed" (1 Pet. 1:6, 7).

FIFTEEN
ANVIL TIME

On God's anvil. Perhaps you've been there.
Melted down. Formless. Undone. Placed on the anvil for . . . reshaping? (A few rough edges too many.) Discipline? ("A good father disciplines.") Testing? (But why so hard?)

I know. I've been on it. It's rough. It's a spiritual slump, a famine. The fire goes out. Although the fire may flame for a moment, it soon disappears. We drift downward. Downward into the foggy valley of question, the misty lowland of discouragement. Motivation wanes. Desire is distant. Responsibilities are depressing.

Passion? It slips out the door.

Enthusiasm? Are you kidding?

Anvil time.

It can be caused by a death, a breakup, going broke, going prayerless. The light switch is flipped off and the room darkens. "All the thoughtful words of help and hope have all been nicely said. But I'm still hurting, wondering. . . ."

On the anvil.

Brought face to face with God out of the utter realization that we have nowhere else to go. Jesus, in the garden. Peter, with a tear-streamed face. David, after Bathsheba. Elijah and the "still, small voice." Paul, blind in Damascus.

Pound, pound, pound.

I hope you're not on the anvil. (Unless you need to be and, if so, I hope you are.) Anvil time is not to be avoided; it's to be experienced. Although the tunnel is dark, it does go through the mountain. Anvil time reminds us of who we are and who God is. We shouldn't try to escape it. To escape it could be to escape God.

God sees our life from beginning to end. He may lead us through a storm at age thirty so we can endure a hurricane at age sixty. An instrument is useful only if it's in the right shape. A dull ax or a bent screwdriver needs attention, and so do we. A good blacksmith keeps his tools in shape. So does God.

Should God place you on his anvil, be thankful. It means he thinks you're still worth reshaping.

SIXTEEN
FOOTPRINTS OF
SATAN

"Once he was approached by a leper, who knelt before him begging his help. 'If only you will,' said the man, 'You can cleanse me.' In warm indignation Jesus stretched out his hand, [and] touched him . . ." (Mark 1:40, 41, New English Bible).

I was in an emergency room late one night last
    week. Victims of Satan filled the halls.
    A child—puffy, swollen eyes. Beaten by her
    father. A woman—bruised cheeks, bloody
    nose. "My boyfriend got drunk and hit me,"
    she said, weeping. An old man—uncon-
    scious and drunk on a stretcher. He drooled
    blood in his sleep.
Jesus saw the victims of Satan, too.
    He saw a leper one day . . . fingers gnarled
    . . . skin ulcerated . . . face disfigured.
And he got indignant . . . angry.
    Not a selfish, violent anger. A *holy* anger . . .
    a controlled frustration . . . a compassionate
    disgust. And it moved him. It moved him to
    action.
I'm convinced that the same Satan stalks today
    causing the hunger in Cambodia . . . the
    confusion in the Mideast . . . the egotism on

the movie screen . . . the apathy in Christ's church. And Satan giggles among the dying.
Dear Father,
   May we never grow so "holy," may we never be so "mature," may we never become so religious that we can see the footprints of Satan and stay calm.

SEVENTEEN
THUMP-THUD,
THUMP-THUD

When a potter bakes a pot, he checks its solidity by pulling it out of the oven and thumping it. If it "sings," it's ready. If it "thuds," it's placed back in the oven.

The character of a person is also checked by thumping.

Been thumped lately?

Late-night phone calls. Grouchy teacher. Grumpy moms. Burnt meals. Flat tires. "You've-got-to-be-kidding" deadlines. Those are thumps. Thumps are those irritating inconveniences that trigger the worst in us. They catch us off guard. Flat-footed. They aren't big enough to be crises, but if you get enough of them, watch out! Traffic jams. Long lines. Empty mailboxes. Dirty clothes on the floor. Even as I write this I'm being thumped. Because of interruptions, it has taken me almost two hours to write these two paragraphs. *Thump. Thump. Thump.*

How do I respond? Do I sing? Or do I thud?

Jesus said that out of the nature of the heart a man speaks (Luke 6:45). There's nothing like a good thump to reveal the nature of a heart. The true character of a person is seen not in momentary heroics, but in the thump-packed humdrum of day-to-day living.

If you have a tendency to thud more than you sing, take heart. There is hope for us "thudders":

1. Begin by thanking God for thumps. I don't mean a half-hearted thank you. I mean a "rejoicing, jumping-for-joy" thank you from the bottom of your heart (James 1:2). Chances are that God is doing the thumping. And he's doing it for your own good. So every thump is a reminder that God is molding you (Heb. 12:8).

2. Learn from each thump. Face up to the fact that you are not "thump-proof." You are going to be tested from now on. Might as well learn from the thumps; you can't avoid them. Look upon each inconvenience as an opportunity to develop patience and persistence. Each thump will help you or hurt you, depending on how you use it.

3. Be aware of "thump-slump" times. Know your pressure periods. For me, Mondays are infamous for causing thump-slumps. Fridays can be just as bad. For all of us there are times during the week that we can anticipate an unusual amount of thumping. The best way to handle

thump-slump times? Head on. Bolster yourself with extra prayer and don't give up.

Remember, no thump is disastrous. All thumps work for good if we are loving and obeying God.

EIGHTEEN
NO MORE
CURTAINS!

". . . the curtain of the temple was
torn in two . . ." (Matt. 27:51).

The annual event always drew a crowd. The priest would solemnly ascend the temple steps, cradling in his arms a lamb. As the people waited outside, he would pass through the great curtain and enter the Holy of Holies. He would kill the lamb upon the altar and pray that the blood would appease God. The sins would be rolled back. And the people would sigh with relief.

A great curtain hung as a reminder of the distance between God and man. It was like a deep chasm that no one could breach. Man on his island . . . quarantined because of sin.

God could have left it like that. He could have left the people isolated. He could have washed his hands of the whole mess. He could have turned back, tossed in the towel, and started over on another planet. He *could* have, you know.

But he didn't.

God himself breached the chasm. In the darkness of an eclipsed sun, he and a Lamb stood in the Holy of Holies. He laid the Lamb on the altar. Not the lamb of a priest or a Jew or a shepherd, but the Lamb of God. The angels hushed as the blood of the Sufficient Sacrifice began to fall on the golden altar. Where had dripped the blood of lambs, now dripped the blood of life.

"Behold the Lamb of God."

And then it happened. God turned and looked one last time at the curtain.

"No more." And it was torn . . . from top to bottom. Ripped in two.

"No more!"

"No more lambs!"

"No more curtain!"

"No more sacrifices!"

"No more separation!"

And the sun came out.

NINETEEN
WHO PUSHES YOUR SWING?

Children love to swing. There's nothing like it. Thrusting your feet toward the sky, leaning so far backward that everything looks upside down. Spinning trees, a stomach that jumps into your throat. Ahh, swinging. . . .

I learned a lot about trust on a swing. As a child, I only trusted certain people to push my swing. If I was being pushed by people I trusted (like Dad or Mom), they could do anything they wanted. They could twist me, turn me, stop me. . . . I loved it! I loved it because I trusted the person pushing me. But let a stranger push my swing (which often happened at family reunions and Fourth of July picnics), and it was *hang on, baby!* Who knew what this newcomer would do? When a stranger pushes your swing, you tense up, ball up, and hang on.

It's no fun when your swing is in the hands of someone you don't know.

Remember when Jesus stilled the storm in Matthew 8? The storm wasn't just a gentle spring rain.

This was a *storm*. Matthew calls the storm a *seismos*, which is the Greek word for earthquake. The waves in this earthquake were so high that the boat was hidden. The Sea of Galilee can create a vicious storm. Barclay tells us that "on the west side of the water there are hills with valleys and gulleys; and when a cold wind comes from the west, these valleys and gulleys act like giant funnels. The wind becomes compressed in them and rushes down upon the lake with savage violence."

No, sir, this was no spring shower. This was a storm deluxe. It was frightening enough to scare the pants (or robes) off of a dozen disciples. Even veteran fishermen like Peter knew this storm could be their last. So, with fear and water on their faces, they ran to wake up Jesus.

They ran to do what? Jesus was asleep? Waves tossing the boat like popcorn in a popper, and Jesus was asleep? Water flooding the deck and soaking the sailors, and Jesus was in dreamland? How in the world could he sleep through a storm?

Simple. He knew who was pushing the swing.

The disciples' knees were knocking because their swing was being pushed by a stranger. Not so with Jesus. He could find peace in the storm.

We live in a stormy world. At this writing, wars rage in both hemispheres of our globe. World conflict is threatening all humanity. Jobs are getting scarce. Money continues to get tight. Families are coming apart at the seams.

Everywhere I look, private storms occur. Family deaths, strained marriages, broken hearts, lonely evenings. We must remember who is pushing the swing. We must put our trust in him. We can't grow fearful. He won't let us tumble out.

Who pushes your swing? In the right hands, you can find peace . . . even in the storm.

TWENTY
JUAN—LUNCH

On Friday, May 7, my calendar reads *Juan—Lunch.*
The lunch date never occurred. Juan killed himself
on Thursday, May 6.

Three weeks earlier Juan had spent a week in our
house. He'd just been dumped by a girl. Dumped
hard. Several times I saw him pull out a picture of
them together, taken on New Year's Eve. She was
in an evening gown, Juan was in a tux. "Boy, that
was life in the big time," he'd said longingly, sadly.

He had tried twice before to kill himself, but had
failed. This time he didn't fail. What makes a fellow
do it? I really wonder. What made him finally get
the courage to do it? Juan had breathed the exhaust
of his own car.

Two days earlier I had run into him at Swenson's
Ice Cream Parlor. He was there with some friends.
We laughed some. He seemed to be doing so well.
(Where do we learn that pain is something we have
to hide?)

What emotions do I feel?

Confusion. The black veil of hopeless death falls viciously. Why? How horrid it is to be governed by laws we don't understand.

Guilt. You see, we were originally scheduled to have lunch on May 6, but I had postponed it to May 7. I can't help but wonder, "What if I hadn't canceled?" But the guilt will pass. I know too well my own failures. The inability to forgive one's self is itself suicidal.

Clarity. How death clears the fog! The abrupt departure of life starkly reminds me of why we are here. Death causes all other preoccupations of life to tumble down the hill, leaving at the top this one priority: Jesus Christ rose from the dead and God has forgiven my failures. When all we have to face is death and all we have to remember are memories, Jesus' victory and God's forgiveness will be the only things that matter.

Why am I writing this? It comforts me, for one thing. For another, I want you to know how terribly vital each person in the world is. I loved Juan. In a small way this is a tribute to him. He was a victim of despair. He wanted a life he couldn't have. He had a life he couldn't handle.

Juan was caught in a shouting match between the world on one side and a handful of us on the other. "Life isn't worth it!" screamed the world. "Yes it is," we yelled back. "No it isn't." "Yes it is!" And there was Juan in the middle, caught and confused. He'd look at us—then at the world. A puppy between two masters. Finally, we were outshouted. "You're right, it isn't worth it!" He despaired and jumped.

But we can't quit shouting. Many may ignore us, but many will hear. And if only one hears, isn't it worth it?

TWENTY-ONE
LIFE FROM THE
PRESSBOX

It made sense, after someone explained it to me, why our high school football coach would always disappear in the middle of the third quarter. I remember during my first game on the varsity squad, I looked up from the sidelines (where I spent most of my time), and noticed that he was gone. (It was a lot quieter.) I couldn't figure out what had happened. I was afraid the other team had kidnapped him. Or maybe he had gotten sick on his chewing tobacco. So I asked a senior "sideliner." (They know everything.)

"Where's the coach?" I asked, thinking I was the only one to notice his absence, which made me feel important.

"In the pressbox," he answered.

"Getting coffee?" I asked.

"No, getting perspective."

Now, that makes sense, doesn't it? There's no way a coach can really keep up with the game from the sidelines. Everyone yelling advice. Parents complaining. Players screaming. Cheerleaders cheering. Sometimes you've got to get away from the game to see it.

Occasionally we need to try that on ourselves, too. How vital it is that we keep a finger on the pulse of our own lives. How critical are those times of self-examination and evaluation. Yet it's hard to evaluate ourselves while we're in the middle of the game: schedules pressing, phones ringing, children crying.

I've got a suggestion. Take some pressbox time. Take some time (at least half a day) and get away from everything and everyone.

Take your Bible and notebook and get a pressbox view of your life. Are you as in tune with God as you need to be? How is your relationship with your mate and children? What about your goals in life? Perhaps some decisions need to be made. Spend much time in prayer. Meditate on God's Word. Be quiet. Fast for the day.

Now, I'm not talking about a get-away-from-it-all day when you shop, play tennis, and relax in the sun. (Although such times are needed, too.) I'm suggesting an intense, soul-searching day spent in reverence before God and in candid honesty with yourself. Write down your life story. Reread God's story. Recommit your heart to your Maker.

I might mention that a day like this won't just happen. It must be made. You'll never wake up and just happen to have a free day on your hands. (Those went out with your braces.) You'll have to pull out the calendar, elbow out a time in the schedule, and take it. Be stubborn with it. You need the time. Your family needs you to take this time.

Getting some pressbox perspective could change the whole ball game.

TWENTY-TWO
THE VALUE OF A
RELATIONSHIP

I used to visit George every Thursday when I lived in Miami. At the time I wasn't sure what kept drawing me to his musty little trailer. But looking back on it now, I think I know.

George had an unusual appearance—a patch over one eye ("I lost it in the war") and not a hair on his head. He was Canadian to the core and always kept the "maple leaf" draped in front of his trailer. Though over sixty, he swam and golfed daily and danced nightly. His voice boomed like a cannon when he talked, and he walked with such a pendulum swagger that he could have cleared a path for a bull.

But there was something much more profound about George that made me want to visit him. One summer day I realized what it was.

It was a hot Miami afternoon when I knocked on his door. He invited me in with his customary "Well, hello, Max! Come on in here!" (He gave every visitor a glass of lemonade and some secret-recipe popcorn.) I stepped into the trailer.

"I've got someone I want you to meet," continued George with his Canadian twang. "My friend, Ralph."

I looked toward the corner. My eyes were still adjusting from the outside sun to the dimly lit trailer. As my vision cleared, I could see Ralph—and I wasn't sure what to think. There was a certain wildness about him—shoulder-length unkempt hair, a chest-length untamed beard. He was at least George's age, probably older. Apparently he didn't know what to think of me, either. His darting eyes sized me up from beneath his salt-and-pepper hair.

My palms began to sweat.

George interrupted the silence. "Sit down, Max. I've got something to show you." I sat on one side of the table while George scooted in next to Ralph, across from me. "My most valued possession is right here."

I looked at his hands and then around the trailer. "Where, George?"

"Right here." George put his big arm around Ralph's bony shoulders. "My most valued possession is my buddy. Ralph."

A new set of wrinkles appeared on Ralph's face as he broke into a toothless grin. Old friends. George and Ralph. Two crusty old travelers on the backcurve of life's circle. They had found life's most precious element—a relationship.

Relationships. America's most precious resource. Take our oil, take our weapons, but don't take what holds us together—relationships. A nation's strength is measured by the premium it puts on its own people. When people value people, an impenetrable web is drawn, a web of vitality and security.

A relationship. The delicate fusion of two human beings. The intricate weaving of two lives; two sets of moods, mentalities, and temperaments. Two intermingling hearts, both seeking solace and security.

A relationship. It has more power than any nuclear bomb and more potential than any promising seed. Nothing will drive a man to greater courage than a relationship. Nothing will spawn greater devotion than a relationship. Nothing will fire the heart of a patriot or purge the cynicism of a rebel like a relationship.

Ah, but George said it best. "My most valued possession is my buddy."

What matters most in life is not what ladders we climb or what ownings we accumulate. What matters most is a relationship.

What steps are you taking to protect your "possessions"? What measures are you using to insure that your relationships are strong and healthy? What are you doing to solidify the bridges between you and those in your world?

Do you resolve conflict as soon as possible, or do you "allow the sun to go down on your wrath"? Do you verbalize your love every day to your mate and children? Do you look for chances to forgive? Do you pray daily for those in your life? Do you count the lives of your family members and friends more important than your own?

Our Master knew the value of a relationship. It was through relationships that he changed the world. His movement thrived not on personality or power, but on championing the value of a person. He built bridges and crossed them. Touching the leper . . . uniting the estranged . . . exalting the prostitute. And what was that he said about loving your neighbor as yourself?

It's a wise man who values people above possessions. Many wealthy men have died paupers because they gave their lives to things and not to people. And many paupers have left this earth in contentment because they loved their neighbors.

"My most valued possession is my buddy."

TWENTY-THREE
HAVE YOU SEEN
JESUS?

One of the most dramatic scenes in the New Testament occurred in a city known as Caesarea Philippi. One would be hard pressed to find a city with more elaborate religious significance than this one.

At least fourteen temples to Baal dotted the community. The Greeks heralded Caesarea Philippi as the home of the great god Pan, the god of nature. Jewish people pointed to the area around Caesarea Philippi as the source of the Jordan River; the significance of the Jordan River to the Jew was immeasurable. The might of Rome was glorified in a glistening marble temple erected in honor of Caesar. In Caesarea Philippi the Romans celebrated Caesar as divine and Rome as holy.

It must have been some city. Every significant nation and religion of the day was seen here: Syrians, Jews, Greeks, Romans. No modern metropolis can compare with Caesarea Philippi.

It was indeed a dramatic picture. In the midst of this carnival of marble columns and golden idols, a penniless, homeless, nameless Nazarene asks his band of followers, "Who do you say that I am?" (Matt. 16:13-16).

The immensity of the question is staggering. I would imagine that Peter's answer did not come without some hesitation. Shuffling of feet. Anxious silence. How absurd that this man should be the Son of God. No trumpets. No purple robes. No armies. Yet there was that glint of determination in his eye and that edge of certainty in his message.

Peter's response sliced the silence. "I believe that you are . . . the Son of God."

Many have looked at Jesus; but few have seen him. Many have seen his shadow, his people, his story. But only a handful have seen Jesus. Only a few have looked through the fog of religiosity and found him. Only a few have dared to stand eye to eye and heart to heart with Jesus and say, "I believe that you are the Son of God."

TWENTY-FOUR
A GOOD HEART,
BUT

. . . .

(Scene—Sunday A.M. assembly; silent prayer)

Max: God, I want to do great things.

God: You do?

Max: You bet! I want to teach millions! I want to fill the Rose Bowl! I want all of the world to know your saving power! I dream of the day. . . .

God: That's great, Max. In fact, I can use you today after church.

Max: Super! How about some radio and TV work or . . . or . . . or an engagement to speak to Congress?

God: Well, that's not exactly what I had in mind. See that fellow sitting next to you?

Max: Yes.

God: He needs a ride home.

Max (quietly): What?

God: He needs a ride home. And while you're at it, one of the older ladies sitting near you is worried about getting a refrigerator moved.

Why don't you drop by this afternoon
and. . . .

Max (pleading): But, God, what about the world?

God (smiling): Think about it.

TWENTY-FIVE
THE HIKER

In the barren prairie, the hiker huddles down. The cold northerly sweeps over him, stinging his face and numbing his fingers. The whistle of the wind is deafening. The hiker hugs his knees to his chest, yearning for warmth.

He doesn't move. The sky is orange with dirt. His teeth are grainy, his eyes sooty. He thinks of quitting. Going home. Home to the mountains.

"Ahh. The mountains." The spirit that moved him in the mountains seems so far away. For a moment, his mind wanders back to his homeland. Green country. Mountain trails. Fresh water. Hikers hiking on well-marked trails. No surprises, few fears, rich companionship.

One day, while on a brisk hike, he had stopped to look out from the mountains across the neighboring desert. He felt strangely pulled to the sweeping barrenness that lay before him. The next day he paused again. And the next, and the next. "Shouldn't someone go there? Shouldn't someone try to take life to the desert?" Slowly the flicker in his heart became a flame.

Many agreed that someone should go, but no one volunteered.

Uncharted land, fearful storms, loneliness.

But the hiker, spurred by the enthusiasm of others, determined to go. After careful preparation, he set out, alone. With the cheers of his friends behind him, he descended the grassy highlands and entered the desolate wilderness.

The first few days his steps were springy and his eye was keen. He yearned to do his part to bring life to the desert. Then came the heat. The scorpions. The monotony. The snakes. Slowly, the fire diminished. And now . . . the storm. The endless roar of the wind. The relentless, cursed cold.

"I don't know how much more I can take." Weary and beaten, the hiker considers going back. "At least I got this far." Knees tucked under him, head bowed, almost touching the ground. "Will it ever stop?"

Grimly he laughs at the irony of the situation. "Some hiker. Too tired to go on, yet too ashamed to go home." Deep, deep is the struggle. No longer can he hear the voices of friends. Long gone is the romance of his mission. No longer does he float on the fancifulness of a dream.

"Maybe someone else should do this. I'm too young, too inexperienced." The winds of discouragement and fear whip at his fire, exhausting what is left of the flame. But the coals remain, hidden and hot.

The hiker, now almost the storm's victim, looks one last time for the fire. (Is there any greater challenge than that of stirring a spirit while in the clutches of defeat?) Yearning and clawing, the temptation to quit is gradually overcome by the urge to go on. Blowing on the coals, the hiker once again hears the call to the desert. Though faint, the call is clear.

With all the strength he can summon, the hiker rises to his feet, bows his head, and takes his first step into the wind.

TWENTY-SIX
THE DAY MY PLATE
WAS BROKEN

It was past midnight in Dalton, Georgia, as I stood in a dimly lit phone booth making a call to my folks. My first summer job away from home wasn't panning out as it was supposed to. The work was hard. My two best friends had quit and gone back to Texas, and I was bunking in the Salvation Army until I could find an apartment.

For a big, tough nineteen-year-old, I sure felt small.

The voices of my mom and dad had never sounded so sweet. And although I tried to hide it, my loneliness was obvious. I had promised my parents that if they'd let me go, I'd stick it out for the whole summer. But now those three months looked like eternity.

As I explained my plight, I could tell my mom wanted me to come home. But just as she said, "Why don't you come . . . ," my dad, who was on the extension, interrupted her. "We'd love for you to come back, but we've already broken your plate."

(That was West Texas talk for "We love you, Max, but it's time to grow up.")

It takes a wise father to know when to push his son out of the nest. It's painful, but it has to be done. I'll always be thankful that my dad gave me wings and then made me use them.

TWENTY-SEVEN
PUTTING YOUR BELIEFS
WHERE YOUR HEART IS

Take a pen and paper and get alone. Go where it's quiet, where you can think. Find a place that will offer you an hour's worth of uninterrupted thinking. Then sit down. Take your pen in your hand and—are you ready?—write down what you believe. Not what you think, or hope, or speculate, but what you *believe*. Put on paper those bedrock convictions that are worth building a life on, that are worth giving a life for.

For example, here are some not-for-sale, non-negotiable undeniables that I believe:

- There is a God whose all-consuming concern is whether or not I love him.
- I have a reason to be alive.
- Money is not the answer. Therefore, the abundance or lack of it will not rule me.
- I will never die.
- My family loves me and I love them.

- I will live forever, and heaven is but a wink away.
- I control my moods . . . not vice versa.
- I can change my world.
- The most important element in the world is another human being.

Now look at your list. Analyze it. What do you think? Is your foundation solid enough to stand on? If not, be patient. Give yourself some time to grow.

Don't throw that list away. Keep it. I've got a special assignment for you. Put your list someplace where you'll always have it. In your wallet, your purse. . . . Somewhere convenient.

The next time you're intimidated by Mr. Know-It-All or by Miss Have-It-All, the next time your self-image limps out the door, pull out your list. Take a long look at it. Have any of your undeniables been threatened? Has your foundation been attacked?

Usually not. Here's the point: if you know what you believe (I mean *really* know it), if you know what's important and what's trivial, then you won't be tied down by all the little Lilliputians in the world.

I *really* believe that.

TWENTY-EIGHT
SOMEDAY

Thousands of years before Jesus was called the Lamb of God, God promised forgiveness.

"Someday," he promised Hosea, "someday I will remember their sins no more."

"Someday," God confided to Jeremiah, "these people will be my people and I will be their God."

"And someday," wrote David, "the mistakes of men will be tossed, not under a rug, or behind the sofa, but far, far away. As far as the east is from the west."

And do you know what? That someday came. On a garbage heap outside of Jerusalem.

Someday the almighty God, who has every right to make me burn forever, will look past my apathy, my gluttony, my lying, and my lusting. He will point to the cross and invite me to come home . . . forgiven . . . forever.

TWENTY-NINE
THE BLUNTED AX

Until the cross, Satan held a cruel ax over man's head. All feared the ax of death. Its eerie glimmer humbled all who faced it. From the greatest to the smallest, all avoided the ax. Satan's mysterious, abrupt blade severed man from the living and cast him into the unknown.

For centuries men had appeased the ax, evaded the ax, ignored the ax. But its razor-sharp edge made victims of all, relentlessly marching each to the chopping block; sweeping down upon mankind an execution that none could escape.

Until the cross. It was at the cross that the power of the ax was dissolved and its true weakness disclosed. With all of the strength that Satan could muster and all the cruelty he could display, he brought the ax down upon the neck of the Son of God. The savage blow rang throughout the forest of death, and echoed across the universe.

"I have done it!" Satan laughed. His wiry figure contorted with laughter. "I have killed life." The triumphant scream echoed in the chambers of

Hades. And for a brief, fearful moment, all humanity gasped.

But the Divine Figure was not to be trapped. His body rose from the block, his head still intact, his life surviving. Jesus had blunted the ax. Jesus had flouted the executioner's threat. Turning to Satan, he posed the question that paved the path to immortality. "Where, O death, is your victory? Where, O death, is your sting?"

THIRTY
VALENTINE'S DAY,
1965

My decision had been made sometime during the week. I didn't tell a soul. (For a ten-year-old, I kept a good secret.) I think I reached my decision on a Monday . . . or maybe Tuesday. Nonetheless, after the decision was made, Sunday took forever to arrive.

But Sunday finally came. *The* Sunday. My Sunday.

Mom didn't have to wake me that day. I was up before her. It just so happened that it was Valentine's Day. I hardly noticed. I remember polishing my "church shoes" until I could see my face in the reflection. An extra palmful of Vitalis was needed on my short red hair to keep my rooster tail from popping up. My daddy tied my tie for me. I washed my face so hard my freckles almost came off.

I was nervous during Sunday school, glad when it was over. Butterflies were swarming in my stomach. The assembly, however, seemed to settle my nervous energy. I sang louder than ever and hung on every word of the sermon. The butterflies stopped. I don't remember questioning the decision. It seemed so obvious, so right.

The invitation song had hardly begun when I made my move. The five or six steps I had to make, I made fast. So fast that no one saw me go forward except those near the front.

I told our preacher I wanted to be baptized into Jesus. With an innocent faith that children so easily have, I asked God to take over. Did I understand all the implications of my conversion? No. All I knew was that Jesus' love awaited those who would respond to it, so I did. Ever since that day the Creator of the world—the almighty God—has watched over me like a daddy over a baby, loving me as I have never deserved and sticking with me when others left.

It was the most beautiful day of my life. What a wonderful Valentine's Day!

THIRTY-ONE
OPEN MANHOLES
AND SUDDEN SIN

It happens in an instant. One minute you are walking and whistling, the next you are wide-eyed and falling. Satan yanks back the manhole cover and an innocent afternoon stroll becomes a horror story. Helplessly you tumble, aware of the fall but unable to gain control. You crash at the bottom and stare blankly into the darkness. You inhale the evil stench and sit in Satan's sewage until he spits you out and you land, dumbfounded and shellshocked, on the sidewalk.

Such is the pattern of sudden sin. Can you relate to it? Very few sins are premeditated and planned. Very few of us would qualify for Satan's strategy team. We spend our time avoiding sin, not planning it. But don't think for one minute that just because you don't want to fall that you won't. Satan has a special trick for you, and he only pulls it out when you aren't looking.

This yellow-bellied father of lies doesn't dare meet you face to face. No, sir. Don't expect this demon of demons to challenge you to a duel. Not this snake. He hasn't the integrity to tell you to turn around and put up your dukes. He fights dirty. He is the master of the trapdoor and the author of weak moments. He waits until your back is turned. He waits until your defense is down. He waits until the bell has rung and you are walking back to your corner. Then he aims his dart at your weakest point and. . . .

Bullseye! You lose your temper. You lust. You fall. You take a drag. You buy a drink. You kiss the woman. You follow the crowd. You rationalize. You say yes. You sign your name. You forget who you are. You walk into her room. You look in the window. You break your promise. You buy the magazine. You lie. You covet. You stomp your feet and demand your way.

You deny your Master.

It's David disrobing Bathsheba. It's Adam accepting the fruit from Eve. It's Abraham lying about Sarah. It's Peter denying that he ever knew Jesus. It's Noah, drunk and naked in his tent. It's Lot, in bed with his own daughter. It's your worst nightmare. It's sudden. It's sin.

Satan numbs our awareness and short-circuits our self-control. We know what we are doing and yet can't believe that we are doing it. In the fog of weakness we want to stop but haven't the will to do so. We want to turn around, but our feet won't move. We want to run and, pitifully, we want to stay.

It's the teenager in the backseat. It's the alcoholic buying "just one." It's the boss touching his secretary's hand. The husband walking into the porn shop. The mother losing her temper. The father beating his child. The gambler losing his money. The Christian losing control. And it's Satan gaining a foothold.

Confusion. Guilt. Rationalization. Despair. It all hits. It hits hard. We numbly pick ourselves up and stagger back into our world. "Oh God, what have I done?" "Should I tell someone?" "I'll never do it again." "My God, can you forgive me?"

No one who is reading these words is free from the treachery of sudden sin. No one is immune to this trick of perdition. This demon of hell can scale the highest monastery wall, penetrate the deepest faith, and desecrate the purest home.

Some of you know exactly what I mean. You could write these words better than I, couldn't you? Some of you, like me, have tumbled so often that the stench of Satan's breath is far from a novelty. You've asked for God's forgiveness so often that you worry that the well of mercy might run dry.

Want to sharpen your defenses a bit? Do you need help in reinforcing your weaponry? Have you tumbled down the manhole once too many times? Then consider the ideas below:

First, *recognize Satan.* Our war is not with flesh and blood but with Satan himself. Do like Jesus did when Satan met him in the wilderness. Call him by name. Rip off his mask. Denounce his disguise. He appears in the most innocent of clothing: a night out with the boys, a good book, a popular movie, a pretty neighbor. But don't let him fool you! When the urge to sin rears its ugly head, look him squarely in the eye and call his bluff. "Get behind me, Satan!" "Not this time, you dog of hell! I've walked your stinking corridors before. Go back to the pit where you belong!" Whatever you do, don't flirt with this fallen angel. He'll thrash you like wheat.

Second, *accept God's forgiveness.* Romans chapter 7 is the Emancipation Proclamation for those of us who have a tendency to tumble. Look at verse 15: "I do not understand what I do. For what I want to do I do not do, but what I hate I do."

Sound familiar? Read on. Verses 18, 19: "For I have the desire to do what is good, but I cannot carry it out. For what I do is not the good I want to do; no, the evil I do not want to do—this I keep on doing."

Man, that fellow has been reading my diary!

"What a wretched man I am! Who will rescue me from this body of death?" (v. 24).

Please, Paul, don't stop there! Is there no oasis in this barrenness of guilt? There is. Thank God and drink deeply as you read verse 25 and verse 1 of chapter 8: "Thanks be to God—through Jesus Christ our Lord! . . . Therefore there is now no condemnation for those who are in Christ Jesus."

Amen. There it is. You read it right. Underline it if you wish. For those *in* Christ there is *no* condemnation. Absolutely none. Claim the promise. Memorize the words. Accept the cleansing. Throw out the guilt. Praise the Lord. And . . . watch out for open manholes.

THIRTY-TWO
WHO'S IN CHARGE
HERE?

Ever have trouble determining God's will for your future? You're not alone. "Do I move to Mobile or Minnesota?" "Do I retire or keep working?" "An engineer at IBM or a clerk at Sears?" "Do I marry or stay single?" The questions are endless. One follows another. Every new responsibility brings new decisions. "What college should my son attend?" "Is it time for children?" "Should I live near the church or commute?"

How in the world do we know what God wants? Do we set out a fleece? Seek advice? Pray? Read the Bible? All these are right, yet there is one decision that must be made first. (Hang on, it's a tough one.)

To know God's will, we must totally surrender to God's will. Our tendency is to make God's decision for him. I used to do that with my mom. As a child, I hated to get the flu for two reasons: (1) it hurt; (2) my mom was a nurse. Since she was an RN, she knew the fastest way to tackle the flu bug was with a needle . . . in my bottom. Ouch! (I grew up thinking penicillin was a dirty word.)

When she would tell me to "go get the medicine," I would get everything but the dreaded needle. I'd come back with an armful: aspirin, Pepto Bismol, ear drops, nose drops, ankle wraps—anything but penicillin. But, as good moms do, she always got her point across. "Now, you know better," she'd say with a smile, and I would go get the (gulp) needle.

Here's the point. Don't go to God with options and expect him to choose one of your preferences. Go to him with empty hands—no hidden agendas, no crossed fingers, nothing behind your back. Go to him with a willingness to do whatever he says. If you surrender your will, then he will "equip you with everything good for doing his will" (Heb. 13:21).

It's a promise.

THIRTY-THREE
"GOD, DON'T YOU CARE?"

"Teacher, don't you care if we
[die]?" (Mark 4:38).

Such an honest cry, a doggedly painful cry. I've asked that one before, haven't you? It's been screamed countless times. . . .

A mother weeps over a stillborn child. A husband is torn from his wife by a tragic accident. The tears of an eight-year-old fall on a daddy's casket. And the question wails.

"God, don't you care?" "Why *me?*" "Why *my* friend?" "Why *my* business?" "Don't you care?"

It's the timeless question. The question asked by literally every person that has stalked this globe. There has never been a president, a worker, or a businessman who hasn't asked it. There has never been a soul who hasn't wrestled with this aching question. Does my God care? Or is my pain God's great goof?

As the winds howled and the sea raged, the impatient and frightened disciples screamed their fear at the sleeping Jesus. "Teacher, don't you care that we are about to die?" He could have kept on sleeping. He could have told them to shut up. He could have impatiently jumped up and angrily dismissed the storm. He could have pointed out their immaturity. . . . But he didn't.

With all the patience that only one who cares can have, he answered the question. He hushed the storm so the shivering disciples wouldn't miss his response. Jesus answered once and for all the aching dilemma of man—"Where is God when I hurt?"

Listening and healing. That's where he is. He cares.

PART THREE
AN INSTRUMENT FOR NOBLE PURPOSES

THIRTY-FOUR
AN INSTRUMENT
FOR NOBLE
PURPOSES

*". . . an instrument for noble
purposes, made holy, useful to the
Master and prepared to do any good
work"* (2 Tim. 2:21).

Ah, to be your instrument, O God,
    like Paul to the Gentiles,
    like Philip to the eunuch,
    like Jesus to the world,
    . . . to be your instrument.
To be like a scalpel in the gentle hands of a surgeon,
    healing and mending.
To be like a plow in the weathered hands of a
  farmer,
    sowing and tending.
To be like a scythe in the sweeping hands of a
  reaper,
    gathering and using.
To be . . . an instrument for noble purposes.
To be honed and tuned,
    in sync with your will,
      sensitive to your touch.
This, my God, is my prayer.
    Draw me from your fire,
    form me on your anvil,
    shape me with your hands,
    and let me be your tool.

THIRTY-FIVE
TODAY I WILL
MAKE A
DIFFERENCE

Today I will make a difference. I will begin by controlling my thoughts. A person is the product of his thoughts. I want to be happy and hopeful; therefore, I will have thoughts that are happy and hopeful. I refuse to be victimized by my circumstances. I will not let petty inconveniences such as stoplights, long lines, and traffic jams be my masters. I will avoid negativism and gossip. Optimism will be my companion, and victory will be my hallmark. Today I will make a difference.

I will be grateful for the twenty-four hours that are before me. Time is a precious commodity. I refuse to allow what little time I have to be contaminated by self-pity, anxiety, or boredom. I will face this day with the joy of a child and courage of a giant. I will drink each minute as though it is my last. When tomorrow comes, today will be gone forever. While it is here, I will use it for loving and giving. Today I will make a difference.

I will not let past failures haunt me. Even though my life is scarred with mistakes, I refuse to rummage through my trash heap of failures. I will admit them. I will correct them. I will press on. Victoriously. No failure is fatal. It's OK to stumble. . . . I will get up. It's OK to fail. . . . I will rise again. Today I will make a difference.

I will spend time with those I love. My spouse, my children, my family. A man can own the world but be poor for the lack of love. A man can own nothing and yet be wealthy in relationships. Today I will spend at least five minutes with the significant people in my world. Five *quality* minutes. Five minutes of talking or hugging or thanking or listening. Five undiluted minutes with my mate, children, and friends.

Today I will make a difference.

THIRTY-SIX
THE TESTED
TUNNEL

We held our breath as he disappeared into the tunnel. There were five of us. Five energetic boys. School was out for the summer so we had turned our attention to the vacant lot next to our house. The flat, West Texas land was a perfect summer playground.

On this particular day it seemed that the attention of the entire world was focused on that tunnel. We had dug a ditch about three feet wide and four feet deep that ran halfway across the lot. To give it the appearance of a tunnel we covered it with several planks of scavenged plywood and a thick layer of dirt. We camouflaged the entrance and exit with a few tumbleweeds and mesquite bushes, and—presto!—we had an underground tunnel. It was ready to entertain an entire neighborhood of ruffians as they fought off Indians, escaped from slavery, and invaded Normandy.

Today was the day we would test the tunnel. Was it strong enough? Wide enough? Would it collapse? Was it deep enough? Was it too long? The only way to find out was to send a volunteer through the tunnel first. (Memory may fail me here, but I think it was my brother who agreed to test the tunnel.)

It was a tense moment. The five of us stood solemnly in our T-shirts and jeans. We gave him last words of encouragement. We patted him on the back. (We admired his self-sacrifice.) We stood quietly as he decisively got down on hands and knees and scurried into the hole. We held our breath as we watched the soles of his high-top sneakers disappear into the darkness.

No one spoke as we waited. The only movement was the pounding of our young hearts. Our eyes stayed fixed on the tunnel exit.

Finally, after we had each died a thousand deaths, my brother's sandy-blond hair emerged from the other end. I can remember his triumphant fist leading the way as he scrambled out, yelling, "There's nothing to it! Don't worry!" And who could argue with the testimony of seeing him alive and well, jumping up and down at the tunnel's exit? We all went in!

There is something about a living testimony that gives us courage. Once we see someone else emerging from life's dark tunnels we realize that we, too, can overcome.

Could this be why Jesus is called our pioneer? Is this one of the reasons that he consented to enter the horrid chambers of death? It must be. His words, though persuasive, were not enough. His promises, though true, didn't quite allay the fear of the people. His actions, *even* the act of calling Lazarus from the tomb, didn't convince the crowds that death was nothing to fear. No. In the eyes of humanity, death was still the black veil that separated them from joy. There was no victory over this hooded foe. Its putrid odor invaded the nostril of every human, convincing them that life was only meant to end abruptly and senselessly.

It was left to the Son of God to disclose the true nature of this force. It was on the cross that the showdown occurred. Christ called for Satan's cards. Weary of seeing humanity fooled by a cover-up, he entered the tunnel of death to prove that there was indeed an exit. And, as the world darkened, creation held her breath.

Satan threw his best punch, but it wasn't enough. Even the darkness of hell's tunnel was no match for God's Son. Even the chambers of Hades couldn't stop this raider. Legions of screaming demons held nothing over the Lion of Judah.

Christ emerged from death's tunnel, lifted a triumphant fist toward the sky, and freed all from the fear of death.

"Death has been swallowed up in victory!"

THIRTY-SEVEN
THE MOVEMENT
THAT WAS
DOOMED TO FAIL

From the start, the movement was doomed to fail. For one thing, it began with just 120 men. Remarkably few, when you consider that their homeland had a population of four million. Besides that, most of the men were illiterate and poor. Blue-collar workers they were; far too ignorant to stage an uprising that could make any difference.

Few, if any, had traveled beyond their own country. They were inexperienced and uncultured. Their nation was oppressed. Their people were weary. Their government was corrupt. Their religion was shallow.

The strategy of the movement was disastrous. No headquarters was ever established. No professional research was ever done. Plans were made by the seat of the pants. The leaders couldn't even agree on the exact definition of their mission.

On top of all of this, the movement was impractical. It was far too extreme and absurd. It demanded too much too soon. It lacked any tact. It was too impatient with traditions. It called for a reversal of social classes. It gave too much leverage to women and minority groups.

The movement was doomed to failure. But it didn't fail. It succeeded. Not only did it succeed, it far surpassed any movement in our world's history. Within thirty years the message of Jesus Christ had entered every port, city, and courtyard of the world. It was infectious. It was a moving organism. People actually died to see it continue.

It should have failed, but it succeeded. And it still succeeds. God's movement will never stop. Some say that the U.S. is a post-Christian nation. That doesn't matter. Others scoff at the absurdity of believing in anything absolute. That won't stop it. Materialism blankets the country. Still the movement will continue. It might be slowed, but it will never be stopped.

The church might bicker and fight. The people might grow crusty with traditions. The leaders may grow nearsighted. But the movement will march on. Nothing will ever stop it. The Judean Commander can't be stilled.

We should fall to our knees in humble gratitude that God has allowed us to participate in such a cause. For this is not the movement of a man. It is the movement of God. That is precisely why what should have failed will never fail. It is the movement of God.

THIRTY-EIGHT
COMMUNICATION
IS MORE THAN
WORDS

There are basically two types of people who engage in conversations: those who want to communicate and those trying to show off. The latter is usually a self-styled expert on everything. He can't resist the temptation to toss his opinion in the ring. He is the fellow who makes a comment in class in order to be noticed by others rather than to learn from others.

The true expert on a topic never needs to put others down in order to elevate himself. Nor does he need to employ foreign technical jargon in communicating with the lay public. Such jargon is useful among professionals, but is basically useless elsewhere.

In religion we have developed our own jargon—words like "salvation," "sanctification," "holiness," and "reconciliation." These are words that are invaluable and significant to us, but they do not always communicate to the non-Christian.

One of the paradoxes of communication is that a word must be understandable to both parties be-

111

fore it is acceptable for use. Just because *you* understand a word or concept doesn't mean that the person with whom you are speaking does. The communicator, then, is responsible to select words that are acceptable to both parties. To use long and lanky words just because they are long and lanky may be impressive, but it's certainly not good communication. To throw words in the air and assume that they will be understood is irresponsible and selfish.

E. H. Hutten tells a beautiful story about Albert Einstein. It's a good example of how the expert who knows his "stuff" has no need or desire to impress others. While at Princeton, Einstein would occasionally attend lectures by scientists who often were somewhat obscure and technical in their expression and presentation. As Hutten relates it, "Einstein would rise after the lecture and ask whether he might put a question. He would then go to the blackboard and begin to explain in simple terms what the lecturer had been talking about. 'I wasn't quite sure I understood you correctly,' he would say with great gentleness, and then would make clear what the lecturer had been unable to convey."

This is what effective communication is all about. Jesus was a master at never assuming that something was communicated just because it was spoken. He employed endless creativity: illustrations, parables, quizzes, questions, case studies, and so on. Aquinas said long ago, "The poor teacher stands where he is and beckons the pupil come to him. The good teacher goes to where the pupil is, takes him and leads him to where he ought to go."

THIRTY-NINE
NON-NEGOTIABLE
LOVE

It was a long summer. I was thirteen, a left-fielder on the local pony-league team. I held the record for the most strikeouts . . . as a batter, not as a pitcher. I went the entire season and got only two hits. Over sixty times at bat and only two hits.

Two hits! That's not even good enough to be called a slump! That's a lot of long walks from the plate to the dugout. It got to the point that my team moaned when my time at bat was called. (The other team cheered.) Pretty tough on the self-image of a thirteen-year-old who had dreams of playing for the Dodgers.

The only thing right that summer was my parents' attitude toward my "slump." They never missed a game. Never. Not once did I look up and see their bleacher seats unoccupied. I was still their boy even if I led the league in strikeouts. Their commitment ran deeper than my performance. They showed me the importance of an unwavering commitment.

The Old Testament contains the beautiful story

of Naomi and Ruth, a mother-in-law and daughter-in-law who both lost their husbands. Naomi, a foreigner in Ruth's homeland, yearns to return to her own country. Ruth, still young and marriageable, displays her loyalty to her mother-in-law by going with her and providing for her well-being. The determination and commitment of Ruth are evident in her words: "Where you go I will go, and where you stay I will stay. Your people will be my people and your God my God. Where you die I will die, and there I will be buried" (Ruth 1:16, 17).

One relationship of this caliber can buoy us through the fiercest storms. It was the Beatles who sang, "Will you still need me, will you still feed me, when I'm sixty-four?" Oh, the agony of being sixty-four (or any age, for that matter) and having no one to care for you or need you. Happy are those who have one companion, one relationship that is not based on looks or performance. Every person is in dire need of at least one faithful friend, or a mate who will look him in the eye and say, "I will never leave you. You may grow old and gray, but I'll never leave you. Your face may wrinkle and your body may ruin, but I'll never leave you. The years may be cruel and the times may be hard, but I'll be here. I will never leave you."

Think for a minute about the people in your world. What do they think of your commitment to them? How would they rate your faithfulness? Does your loyalty ever waver? Do you have one person with whom your "contract" is non-negotiable?

Once, two friends were fighting together in a war. The combat was ferocious and many lives were being taken. When one of the two young soldiers was injured and could not get back to the trenches, the other went out to get him, against his officer's orders. He returned mortally wounded and his friend, whom he had carried back, was dead.

The officer looked at the dying soldier, shook his head, and said, "It wasn't worth it."

The young boy, overhearing the remark, smiled and said, "But it *was* worth it, sir, because when I got to him he said, 'Jim, I knew you'd come.'"

Make the most of your relationships. Follow the advice of Benjamin Franklin: "Be slow in choosing friends and be even slower in leaving them."

FORTY
SINGLEHOOD: MISTAKE OR MISSION?

In our culture we have certain things that we simply don't know how to handle: nuclear reactors, inflation, pornography, and, perhaps the most confusing of all, single people.

Single people. What an enigma! Those unusual creatures without wives or husbands. What do you say to them? How can you carry on a conversation with people who are so deprived and socially amputated? Do you pity them? Encourage them? Ignore them? Our culture is built so much around the home that those without a home are . . . well, they're kind of like a plane without a hangar (high-flying, but nowhere to go in a storm).

Once, before I was married, I took a trip to visit my old alma mater. I saw a lot of old friends. Married friends, professors, ex-classmates, ministers, old girl friends. Their response to my still-mate-lessness was amusing.

"Haven't found the right one yet?" they'd inquire. "Gee, Max, I'm sorry." (As though I'd failed at life.)

Some were more tactful. "How's your social life?" (What they really wanted was a scouting report.)

"Fine," I'd say. (I got a kick out of leaving them wondering.)

"Oh." They'd get nervous and then close in with something more discreet: "What about Saturday nights?" Wink.

Others had pity on me. Several put their arms around my shoulders or gently took my hand (as though I were terminally ill) and confided, "God has one waiting for you, Max. Don't be afraid." (Was it my imagination or did I detect a little sympathetic rubbing on the ringless finger?)

I know people mean well. But, honestly . . . is bachelorhood really a disease? Are life and meaning found only at the marriage altar? Is there no room at the inn for those who sleep alone? Are they that socially underdeveloped?

Jesus suggested that singleness is more than acceptable. In fact, Jesus called it a gift (Matt. 19:11); not for everybody, but for a few. A gift that encourages "undivided devotion to the Lord" (1 Cor. 7:35). Perhaps, then, a single Christian should not be regarded as one who is spiritually impotent, but as one who is gifted. I was grateful for my "gift" of singleness. Later God chose to replace my gift with a wife. I'm thankful, and I'm still serving him. But, believe it or not, it is possible to be content and come home to an empty apartment.

Being mateless is not nearly as bad as it's made out to be. In fact, it could be part of a plan.

FORTY-ONE
THE POISON
TONGUE

I once knew an extremely courageous lady. She was courageous for several reasons. For one thing, she was waging an uphill battle against alcoholism. For another, she was doing all she could to restore her relationship with God. It's tough to start over. It's even tougher to start over when people won't let you.

She chose a small church to attend, a church where she knew many members. She thought she'd be received there. One Sunday she parked her car near the church building and got out. As she walked toward the front door, she overheard two ladies talking nearby. The stinging words were not meant for her ears, but she heard them anyway.

"How long is that alcoholic going to hang around here?"

She turned and went back to the car. She never entered another church building until she died. Those ladies meant no harm, yet seemingly painless gossip did irreparable damage.

These five ideas will help us control our tongues:

1. Never say anything about someone that you wouldn't say to his face.
2. Never say anything about someone unless he is there to respond.
3. Refuse to listen to someone else's gossip.
4. Initiate positive statements about people who you're discussing.
5. Remember, "The tongue . . . is a fire" (James 3:6).

FORTY-TWO
THE DAY OF THE QUESTION. *THE* QUESTION!

The day began simply enough. Saturday morning. I slept an hour later than usual. The morning sun greeted my slow-opening eyes. In groggy semi-consciousness I rolled over, enjoying the slower weekend pace. "Heaven will be an eternal Saturday morning. . . ." Fantasy.

Then I remembered. My eyes popped open. "Today is the day." I swallowed hard. The day of the question. THE question. It turned out to be quite a day. In fact, I've never had a day quite like it.

Twilight zone. Dream world. Did I shower? I don't remember. We had breakfast. Went shopping. I was in and out of reality. Dazed (like I felt when I got my bell rung in college intramural football. "Duh . . . yeah, I think I'm Max.")

All day I felt as if I were in Oz or Disney World. I kept waiting for a commercial to yank me back into reality. Silly symptoms of love that I'd often thought foolish, I now experienced. Sweaty palms. Stuttering. Exuberance. Disbelief.

The day of the question. *The* question. She didn't

121

know. At least I didn't tell her. (Turns out, however, that she expected it. She knew it was coming before I did.)

At T minus one hour and counting, I prayed again, as I was driving home from the jewelers (*the* jewelers, with *the* ring). "Lord, we're running out of time. If you don't want me to do it . . . wreck this van!" He didn't.

We had Chinese food at my apartment. The butterflies in my stomach weren't too hungry, so I didn't eat much. After dinner we sat on the couch. My arm hit a plant on the windowsill over our heads. It fell on top of her. Romantic, huh? Boy, I felt stupid.

We sat down to dessert. I had put my proposal in a fortune cookie. The world stopped as she began to read it. The angels stopped singing to listen. As she opened it, she began to cry. *Uh, oh,* I worried, *I've done something wrong.*

But she said yes.

Had I the pen of a magician I couldn't describe my feelings at that moment. I was overwhelmed. Euphoric. Elated. Yet humbled that one so special could return my love. And grateful—that God would give me such a gift.

FORTY-THREE
FIVE VOTES OF
CONFIDENCE

Today is a new day. Hence,

1. I refuse to be shackled by yesterday's failures.
2. What I don't know will no longer be an intimidation; it will be an opportunity.
3. I will not allow people to define my
   mood,
      method,
         image,
            or mission.
4. I will pursue a mission greater than myself by making at least one person happy he saw me.
5. I will have no time for
   self-pity,
      gossip,
         or negativism . . . from myself or from others.

FORTY-FOUR
THE WEDDING
PRAYER

Create in us a love, O Lord.
    An eternal love . . .
    Your love.
    A love that forgives
        any failure,
    spans
        any distance,
    withstands
        any tempest.
Create in us a love, O Lord.
    A new love.
    A fresh love.
    A love with the tenderness
        of a lamb,
    the grandeur
        of a mountain,
    the strength
        of a lion.
    And make us one. Intimately one.
As you made a hundred colors into one sunset
    A thousand cedars into one forest

and countless stars into one galaxy . . .
make our two hearts as
one,
Father, forever . . .
that you may be praised, Father,
forever.

FORTY-FIVE
SARAH

Sarah sat alone. Her hands, freckled with age, rested in her lap. She wore her finest dress. Her nursing-home room spoke of springtime: daisies in the vase, a poinsettia tree blooming outside her window.

"Sundays are special, you know."

Her nursing-home wall spoke of family: an enlargement of grandson Jason hugging Brando the terrier; a framed portrait of her son Jerry, the dentist, and his family in Phoenix; Sarah and her late husband cutting their fortieth wedding anniversary cake. "It would have been fifty years next May."

Sarah sat alone. "They came last Christmas," she said brightly (as if defending her family).

A telegram and a birthday card were taped to the dresser mirror. A church group sang hymns down the hall. She had done her best to make the small room look homey, but a person can only do so much.

A thousand miles away a family played.

Sarah is not sick or ugly. She is not useless or

decrepit. Sarah is simply old. Sarah is not senile, though at times, she confesses, the naiveté of senility is tempting. She doesn't suffer from cancer or arthritis. She hasn't had a stroke. No, her "disease" is much more severe. She suffers from rejection.

Our society has little room for the aged. People like Sarah come in scores. No one intentionally forgets them. Maybe that's why it is so painful. If there were a reason: a fight, a mistake, a dispute. . . . But usually it's unintentional.

Unintentional rejection. It will kill Sarah; she'll die of loneliness. It doesn't matter how nice the convalescent home is; nurses and old folk don't replace a grandbaby's smile or a son's kiss.

Spend all your love on her now.
Forget not the hands, though spotted,
The hair, though thinning,
The eyes, though dim.
For they are a part of you.
And when they are gone, a part of you is gone.

"They came last Christmas," Sarah said with a sigh.

FORTY-SIX
THE SONAR FISH
FINDER

I'm not one to complain about new inventions that make life easier. I love our toasters, hair dryers, calculators. I think they make the little snags smoother in our day-to-day rituals. Yes, I like new ideas. . . . But this time we've gone a little bit far.

It's called the sonar fish finder, and it looks like a hair dryer. You put the nose end under the water and pull the trigger. A digital board responds to sensors on the hose, which in turn respond to the presence of fish. Gotcha! The poor little gilled creatures are victims of a radar system as advanced as anything used in World War II.

But the real loser isn't the fish. It's the fisherman.

I haven't done a lot in my life, but one thing I have done is fish. My father is hooked on fishing. In fact, I can't remember a single vacation during which we didn't fish. Our fishing was as consistent as Hank Aaron's bat. Hours on end. Riverbanks. Trout jumping. "Shhh, you'll scare the fish." Wet tennis shoes. Corks bobbing. Up early. Fifteen horsepower motor. Minnows. Worms. Hooks.

Stringers. Photographs. And man-to-man talks. (A fishing pole does wonders for conversation.) You name it, we talked about it. Football, girls, school . . . God. There's always time to talk when fishing. You see, it never really matters if you catch any fish. Oh, sure, that's what everyone asks you. "What did you catch?" But the beauty of fishing is not in the catch; it's in the experience.

And a sonar fish finder? Well, it almost seems irreverent. It's like a do-it-yourself wedding, or computerized dating. It's like electronic pitchers (dads are supposed to do *that*, too!), or those false logs you put in a fireplace.

Fishing is one of those sacred times that must not be violated and cannot be duplicated.

What is your sacred time? Afternoon walks with your friend? Early morning coffee with your wife? Long drives with your son? An afternoon at the beach with your daughter?

Maybe I'm making too big a deal about the fish finder. Then again, maybe not. The point is this: people are priceless. We should never allow a gadget to interfere with the precious simplicity of waiting for the fish to bite. If my father and I had bought a sonar fish finder we'd have caught more fish, but countless precious conversations would have never existed.

My dad. The greatest fisherman in the world? Probably not. The greatest father? You'd better believe it.

FORTY-SEVEN
TRIUMPHANT . . .
FOREVER!

Triumph is a precious thing. We honor the triumphant. The gallant soldier sitting astride his steed. The determined explorer returning from his discovery. The winning athlete holding aloft the triumphant trophy of victory. Yes, we love triumph.

Triumph brings with it a swell of purpose and meaning. When I'm triumphant, I'm worthy. When I'm triumphant, I count. When I'm triumphant, I'm significant.

Triumph is fleeting, though. Hardly does one taste victory before it is gone; achieved, yet now history. No one remains champion forever. Time for yet another conquest, another victory. Perhaps this is the absurdity of Paul's claim: "But thanks be to God, who always leads us in triumphal procession . . ." (2 Cor. 2:14).

The triumph of Christ is not temporary. "Triumphant in Christ" is not an event or an occasion. It's not fleeting. To be triumphant in Christ is a lifestyle . . . a state of being! To triumph in Christ is not something we do, it's something we are.

Here is the big difference between victory in Christ and victory in the world: A victor in the world rejoices over something he did—swimming the English Channel, climbing Everest, making a million. But the believer rejoices over who he is— a child of God, a forgiven sinner, an heir of eternity. As the hymn goes, ". . . heir of salvation, purchase of God, born of his Spirit, washed in his blood."

Nothing can separate us from our triumph in Christ. Nothing! Our triumph is not based upon our feelings, but upon God's gift. Our triumph is based not upon our perfection, but upon God's forgiveness. How precious is this triumph! For even though we are pressed on every side, the victory is still ours. Nothing can alter the loyalty of God.

A friend of mine recently lost his father to death. The faith of his father had for years served as an inspiration for many. In moments alone with the body of his father, my friend said this thought kept coming to his mind as he looked at his daddy's face: "You won. You won. You won!" As Joan of Arc said when she was abandoned by those who should have stood by her, "It is better to be alone with God. His friendship will not fail me, nor his counsel, nor his love. In his strength I will dare and dare and dare until I die."

"Triumphant in Christ." It is not something we do. It's something we are.

FORTY-EIGHT
THE MAKINGS OF
A MOVEMENT

Each of us should lead a life stirring enough to start a movement. We should yearn to change the world. We should love unquenchably, dream unfalteringly, and work unceasingly.

We should close our ears to the manifold voices of compromise and perch ourselves on the branch of truth. We should champion the value of people, proclaim the forgiveness of God, and claim the promise of heaven.

And we should lead a life stirring enough to cause a movement.

Will we see a movement occur? Perhaps, and perhaps not. Movements never run their course in one generation. The great revivals and reformations that dot the history of humanity were never the work of just one person. Every movement is the sum of visionaries who have gone before, generations of uncompromised lives and non-negotiated truths. Faithful men who have led forceful lives.

Undoubtedly there have been many with Luther's wisdom, or Paul's oratory, of whom we've heard nothing. Maybe an unknown butcher in Greece, a cobbler in France, a mechanic in Idaho. Men with godly lives that form a part of the foundation of a movement.

A movement comes of age when one life harvests the seeds planted by countless lives in previous generations. A movement occurs when one person, no greater or lesser than those who have gone before, lives a forceful life in the fullness of time. Never think that the great movements of Luther, Calvin, or Campbell were entirely of their own doing. They were simply forceful lives placed by God in a receptive crevice of history.

Let's live lives stirring and forceful enough to cause a movement. A true mark of a visionary is his willingness to lay down his life for those whom he'll never see.

Will that movement come in our generation? I hope so. But even if it doesn't, even if we never see it, it will occur. And we'll be a part of it.

CONCLUSION:
EMERGING FROM
THE ANVIL

FORTY-NINE
OFF THE ANVIL

As I type the conclusion of this book, my thoughts are freshly stirred. My wife and I have just returned from an emergency trip to the United States to be with my father. He is very ill. He suffers from Lou Gehrig's disease, a muscle crippler for which there is no known cause or cure. We were called home, not knowing if he would be alive when we arrived. He was, and still is. Yet, even though he has made significant improvement, we know, and he knows, that his time is nearing.

Dad is a man of extreme faith. An able teacher and a strong leader, he never left any doubt as to where he stood on the question of God. His first words to us as we saw him in the intensive care unit were, "I'm ready to go to heaven. I think it's my time."

When the disease was first diagnosed, my wife and I were in the final stages of preparing to do mission work in Rio de Janeiro, Brazil. When I learned that Daddy had a terminal disease, I wrote him, volunteering to change my plans and stay near him. He immediately wrote back, saying, "Don't be concerned about me. I have no fear of death or eternity; just go . . . please him."

My father's life is an example of a heart melted in the fire of God, formed on his anvil, and used in his vineyard. He knew, and knows, what his life was for. In a society of question and confusion, his was one life that had a definition.

Time on God's anvil should do that for us; it should clarify our mission and define our purpose. When a tool emerges from a blacksmith's anvil, there is no question as to what it is for. There is no question as to why it was made. One look at the tool and you instantly know its function. You pick up a hammer and you know that it was made to hit nails. You pick up a saw and you know that it was made to cut wood. You see a screwdriver and you know that it is for tightening screws.

As a human being emerges from the anvil of God, the same should be true. Being tested by God reminds us that our function and task is to be about his business; that our purpose is to be an extension of his nature, an ambassador of his throneroom, and a proclaimer of his message. We should exit the shop with no question as to why God made us. We know our purpose.

In a world of confused identity, in a world of wavering commitments and foggy futures, let us be firm in our role. Society is in dire need of a quorum of people whose task is clear and whose determination is unquenchable.

God has not hidden his will from his people. Our Master does not play games with us. We know who we are. We know what we are for. There may be a question now and then about how and with whom we should carry out his mission. But the underlying truth is still the same. We are God's people and we are to be about his business.

If we live our lives in this way, then we can, like my father, enter into our final years with the assurance of knowing that life was well spent and that heaven is but a wink away.

And is there any greater reward than this?